Contents

The Choices Approach to Historical Turning Points	ii
Note to Teachers	1
Integrating this Unit into Your Curriculum	2
Reading Strategies and Suggestions	3
Day One: Political Geography of Africa	4
Optional Lesson: Source Analysis: Different Perspectives on a Violent Encounter	15
Day Two: Photo Analysis: Look Again	20
Optional Lesson: Kikuyu Fable: A Tale of Resistance	29
Day Three: The Four Case Studies: Organization and Preparation	32
Day Four: The Four Case Studies: Presentation and Discussion	35
Day Five: The All-African People's Conference, Accra, Ghana, 1958	36
Assessment Using Documents	48
Key Terms	53
Issues Toolbox	54
Making Choices Work in Your Classroom	55
Assessment Guide for Oral Presentations	57
Alternative Three-Day Lesson Plan	58

THE CHOICES PROGRAM is a program of the Watson Institute for International Studies at Brown University. CHOICES was established to help citizens think constructively about foreign policy issues, to improve participatory citizenship skills, and to encourage public judgement on policy issues.

The Watson Institute for International Studies was established at Brown University in 1986 to serve as a forum for students, faculty, visiting scholars, and policy practitioners who are committed to analyzing contemporary global problems and developing initiatives to address them.

© Copyright January 2014. First edition. The Choices Program. All rights reserved.
ISBN 1-60123-150-4 TRB/ 978-1-60123-150-5 TRB.

The Choices Approach to Historical Turning Points

Choices curricula are designed to make complex international issues understandable and meaningful for students. Using a student-centered approach, Choices units develop critical thinking and an understanding of the significance of history in our lives today—essential ingredients of responsible citizenship.

Teachers say the collaboration and interaction in Choices units are highly motivating for students. Studies consistently demonstrate that students of all abilities learn best when they are actively engaged with the material. Cooperative learning invites students to take pride in their own contributions and in the group product, enhancing students' confidence as learners. Research demonstrates that students using the Choices approach learn the factual information presented as well as or better than those using a lecture-discussion format. Choices units offer students with diverse abilities and learning styles the opportunity to contribute, collaborate, and achieve.

Choices units on historical turning points include student readings, primary sources, suggested lesson plans, resources for structuring cooperative learning, role plays, and simulations. Students are challenged to:

- understand historical context
- analyze and evaluate multiple perspectives at a turning point in history
- analyze primary sources that provide a grounded understanding of the moment
- understand the internal logic of a viewpoint
- identify the conflicting values represented by different points of view
- develop and articulate original viewpoints
- recognize relationships between history and current issues
- communicate in written and oral presentations
- collaborate with peers

Choices curricula offer teachers a flexible resource for covering course material while actively engaging students and developing skills in critical thinking, persuasive writing, and informed citizenship. The instructional activities that are central to Choices units can be valuable components in any teacher's repertoire of effective teaching strategies.

Historical Understanding

Each Choices curriculum resource provides students with extensive information about a historical issue. Choices units help students to understand that historical events often involved competing and highly contested views. The Choices approach emphasizes that historical outcomes were hardly inevitable. This approach helps students to develop a more sophisticated understanding of history.

Each Choices unit presents the range of views that were considered at a turning point in history. Students understand and analyze these views through a role-play activity. The activity demands analysis and evaluation of the conflicting values, interests, and priorities.

The final reading in a Choices historical unit presents the outcome of the turning point and reviews subsequent events.

Note to Teachers

In the late nineteenth century, European powers claimed the African continent for themselves. In the guise of a humanitarian mission, European leaders and businesses exploited African natural resources and people to fuel European economic development. But Africans did not submit to outside control willingly. In fact, African resistance continued throughout the colonial period, culminating in the independence movements of the mid-twentieth century. *Colonization and Independence in Africa* explores these topics generally, as well as through four country case studies: Ghana, Algeria, Kenya, and the Democratic Republic of the Congo. A central activity uses primary sources to examine different perspectives on colonization and decolonization in these four countries. The reading culminates with a discussion of colonialism's legacies for the African continent.

Suggested Five-Day Lesson Plan: The Teacher Resource Book accompanying *Colonization and Independence in Africa* contains day-by-day lesson plans and student activities that use primary source documents and help build critical-thinking skills. You may also find the "Alternative Three-Day Lesson Plan" useful.

• **Alternative Study Guides:** Each section of reading is accompanied by two study guides. The standard study guide helps students gather the information in the readings in preparation for analysis and synthesis in class. It also lists key terms that students will encounter in the reading. The advanced study guide requires that students analyze and synthesize material prior to class activities.

• **Vocabulary and Concepts:** The reading in *Colonization and Independence in Africa* addresses subjects that are complex and challenging. To help your students get the most out of the text, you may want to review with them "Key Terms" on page TRB-53 before they begin their assignment. An "Issues Toolbox" is also included on page TRB-54. This provides additional information on key concepts of particular importance.

• **Additional Resources:** Further resources can be found at <www.choices.edu/colonizationmaterials>.

The lesson plans offered in *Colonization and Independence in Africa* are provided as a guide. Many teachers choose to adapt or devote additional time to certain activities. We hope that these suggestions help you in tailoring the unit to fit the needs of your classroom.

Integrating this Unit into Your Curriculum

Units produced by the Choices Program can be integrated into a variety of social studies courses. Below are a few ideas about where *Colonization and Independence in Africa* might fit into your curriculum.

World History: *Colonization and Independence in Africa* focuses on four major themes in world history—imperialism, colonialism, decolonization, and nation-state formation. Examining European colonialism and the struggle for independence on the African continent helps students gain a greater understanding of Africa's history. The economic exploitation, discrimination, and violent oppression that frequently accompanied colonial rule is covered. Africans' varied methods of resistance are also given particular attention.

Following World War II, independence movements swept the globe. The readings and lessons of *Colonization and Independence in Africa* explore this moment in time, specifically Africans' demands for self-governance and the process of achieving independence.

International Relations: In recent years, political battles have pitted wealthy countries (including industrialized countries and the former Soviet bloc) against newly-industrializing and poorer countries. Although the geographic terminology is not perfect, experts often refer to these two groups of countries as the global "North" and the global "South." North-South issues have deep historical roots. During the nineteenth and early twentieth centuries, the leading countries of what is today the global North competed to establish colonies in Africa and other regions to gain access to raw materials and open up new markets for their manufactured goods. Although almost all of the colonies under European control gained independence by the 1960s, the impact of colonialism has continued to influence international relations. Economic links between the former colonies and the former imperial powers remain important. In addition, leaders of the global South argue that colonialism is the source of many of the problems that currently afflict their countries.

Reading Strategies and Suggestions

This curriculum covers a wide range of issues over a long period of time. Your students may find the readings complex. It might also be difficult for them to synthesize such a large amount of information. The following are suggestions to help your students better understand the readings.

Pre-reading strategies: Help students to prepare for the reading.

1. You might create a Know/Want to Know/Learned (K-W-L) worksheet for students to record what they already know and what they want to know about the history of African colonization and independence. As they read, they can fill out the "learned" section of the worksheet. Alternatively, brainstorm their current knowledge, and then create visual maps in which students link the concepts and ideas they have about the topic.

2. Use the questions in the text to introduce students to the topic. Ask them to scan the reading for major headings, images, and questions so they can gain familiarity with the structure and organization of the text.

3. Preview the vocabulary and key concepts listed on each study guide and in the back of the TRB with students. The study guides ask students to identify key terms from the reading that they do not know. Establish a system to help students find definitions for these key terms.

4. Since studies show that most students are visual learners, use a visual introduction, such as photographs or a short video, to orient your students.

5. Be sure that students understand the purpose for their reading the text. Will you have a debate later, and they need to know the information to formulate arguments? Will they create a class podcast or blog?

Split up readings into smaller chunks: Assign students readings over a longer period of time or divide readings among groups of students.

Graphic organizers: You may also wish to use graphic organizers to help your students better understand the information that they are given. These organizers are located on TRB-8, TRB-25, and TRB-40. In addition, a graphic organizer for the four case studies is provided on TRB-34. Students can complete them in class in groups or as part of their homework, or you can use them as reading checks or quizzes.

Political Geography of Africa

Objectives:
Students will: Practice general map reading skills.

Explore the geography of Africa.

Compare the African continent today with the political geography of the late nineteenth century and early twentieth century.

Required Reading:
Before beginning the lesson, students should have read the Introduction and Part I of the student text and completed "Study Guide—Introduction and Part I" (TRB 5-6) or "Advanced Study Guide—Introduction and Part I" (TRB-7).

Handouts:
"Africa Today" (TRB 9-10)

"Africa in the Late Nineteenth Century" (TRB 11-12)

"Africa in 1914" (TRB 13-14)

Note:
This exercise is designed to acquaint students with the basic political geography covered in the reading. Teachers may want students to refer to their maps as they continue reading.

In the Classroom:
1. Reviewing Major Concepts—Write the following on the board: "What is colonialism?" Ask students to come up with a definition, and write their answers on the board.

Using the reading in Part I, have students explain what they know about Africa prior to 1880. In what ways were communities in Africa connected to each other? To the outside world? What developments were happening in some parts of the continent in the nineteenth century? Be sure to emphasize to students the diversity of people, events, and experiences across the continent. Why is it difficult to make generalizations about African history?

Now ask students to consider the Berlin Conference and the colonization of Africa by European countries. Why were some European leaders interested in claiming territory in Africa? How did African communities respond? What were some ways that colonial rule affected people in Africa?

2. Group Work—Form small groups and distribute the three handouts. Ask students to note the different dates on the maps. Each group should carefully review the maps and answer the questions that follow.

3. Making Connections—When groups finish, ask them to share their findings with the class. Using the maps and their knowledge of this history, ask students to describe the ways in which European colonialism changed the societies, economies, governments, and religious practices of people living in Africa.

Ask students to think of other examples from history in which outside powers took control of other countries or territories. Is this something that could happen today?

Homework:
Students should read Part II of the student text and complete "Study Guide—Part II" (TRB 22-23) or "Advanced Study Guide—Part II" (TRB-24).

Name:_____

Colonization and Independence in Africa
Day One
TRB 5

Study Guide—Introduction and Part I

Vocabulary: Be sure that you understand these key terms from the Introduction and Part I of your reading. Circle ones that you do not know.

colonialism
colonial system
economic development
culture
agriculturalists
sovereignty
trade routes

exported
textiles
abolition
ideologies
ethnicities
treaties

missionary
guerilla warfare
cash crops
infrastructure
assimilation
indirect rule

Questions:

1. What aspects of history did Europeans emphasize about the colonial period in Africa? What aspects of this history did they leave out?

2. Define colonialism in your own words.

3. List three beliefs, goods, or cultural practices that were exchanged through trade routes on the African continent.
    a.

    b.

    c.

4. How did the slave trade affect local African communities?

5. In 1880, about ____ percent of Africa was _____. By 1900, _____ had laid claim to all but the African territories of _____ and _____.

WWW.CHOICES.EDU ■ WATSON INSTITUTE FOR INTERNATIONAL STUDIES, BROWN UNIVERSITY ■ THE CHOICES PROGRAM

Colonization and Independence in Africa — Day One

Name:_____

6. What were two reasons why European governments became interested in controlling parts of Africa?
   a.

   b.

7. What was the purpose of the Berlin Conference of 1884-1885?

8. List two examples of ways Africans resisted European control.
   a.

   b.

9. List two colonies and describe how their economies changed under colonial rule.
   a.

   b.

10. Describe how Britain and France governed their colonies.
    Britain:

    France:

11. How did European rule alter the position of women in many African colonies?

Name:_____

Advanced Study Guide—Introduction and Part I

1. How was the African continent connected to other regions of the world prior to colonial rule?

2. What motivated European powers to take control of Africa in the late nineteenth century?

3. Who was present at the Berlin Conference of 1884-1885? Whose views were not represented? How did this influence the decisions made at the conference?

4. How did colonial economic policies affect Africans?

Part I Graphic Organizer

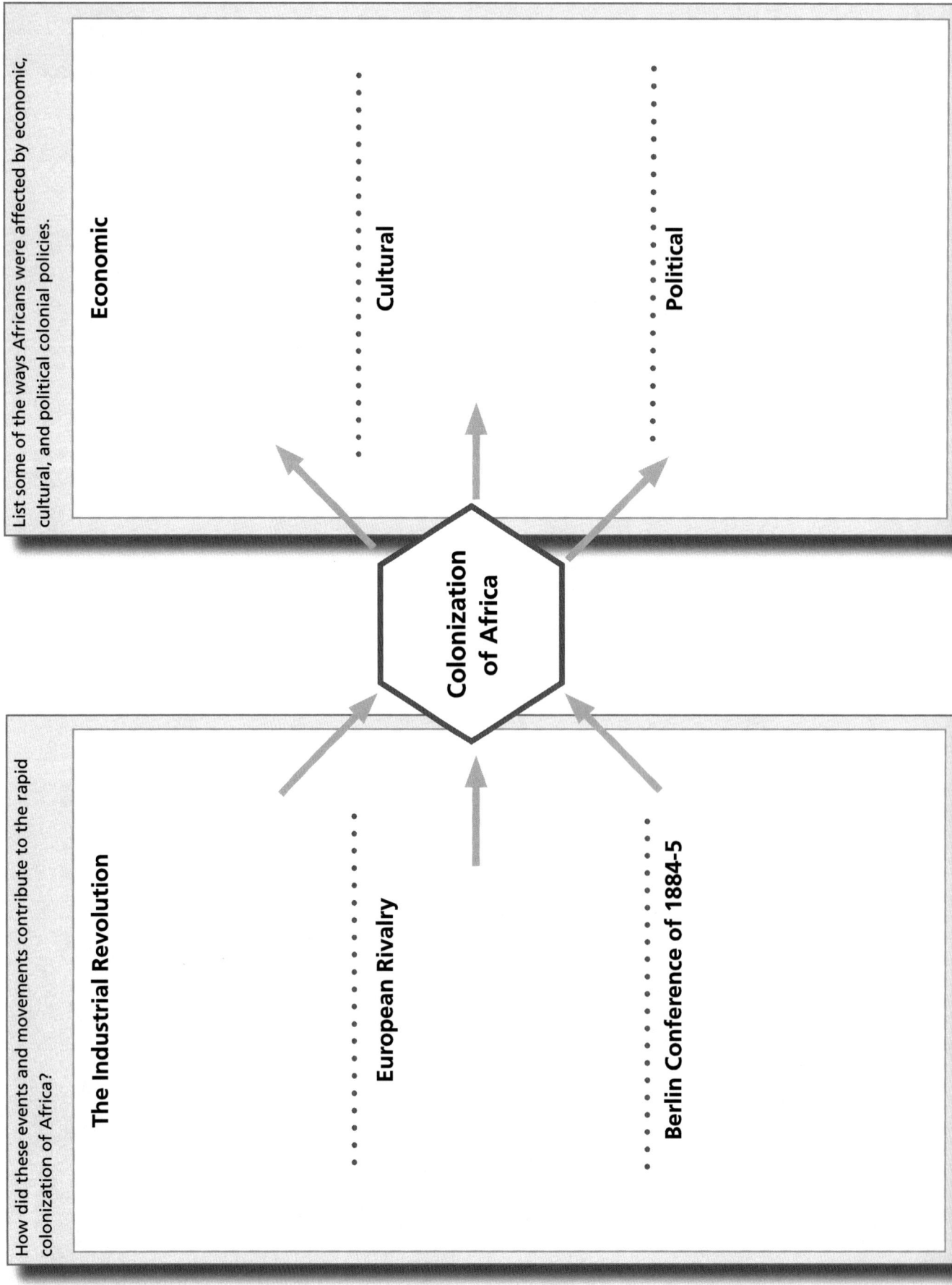

Name:_____

Africa Today

Instructions: Use the map to answer the questions that follow.

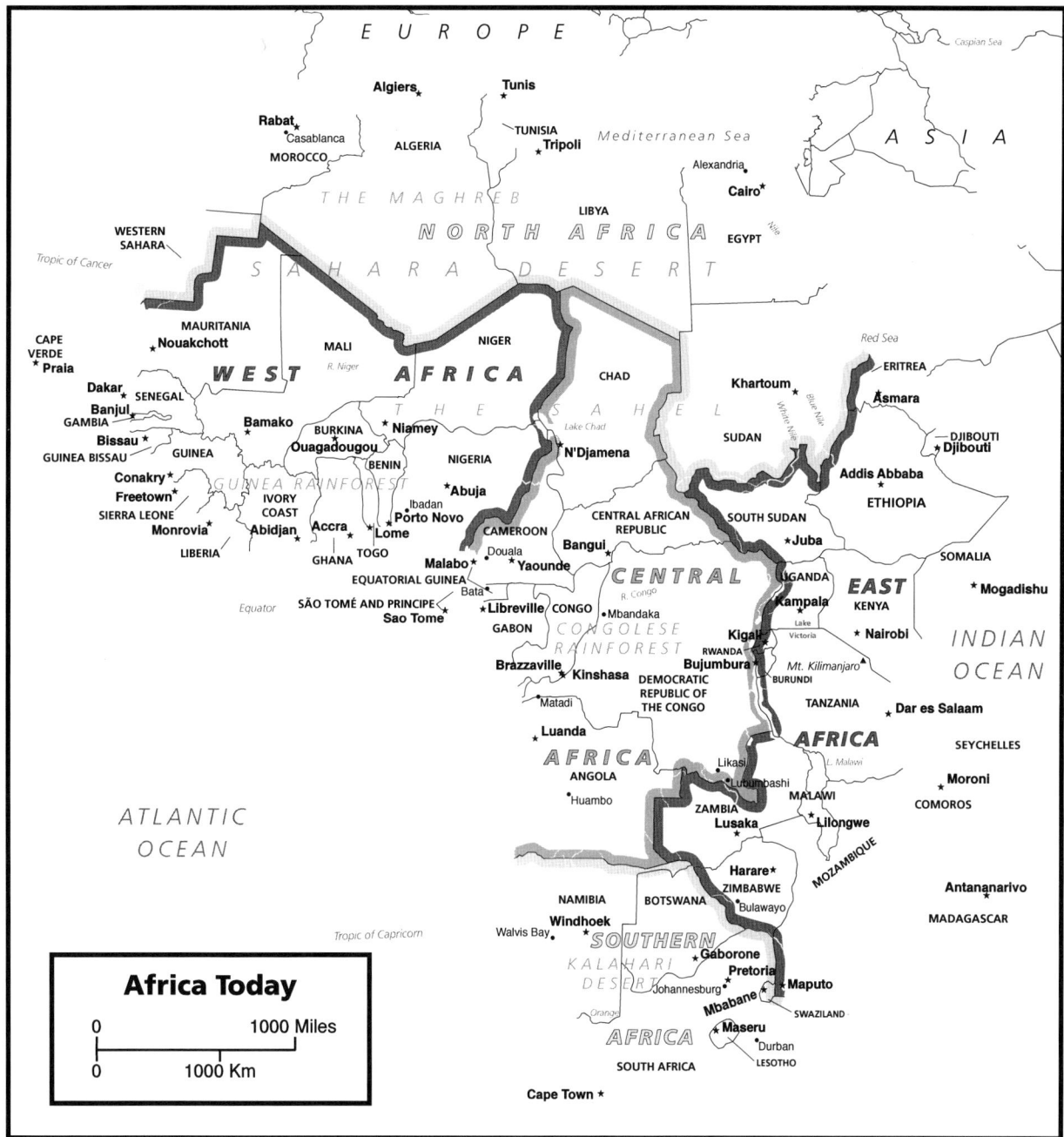

Questions:
1. Which major bodies of water border Africa?

Name:_____

2. Which two continents are closest to Africa?

3. List three major topographical features on the African continent (for example, the names of major rivers, deserts, or forests).
   a.

   b.

   c.

4. List three countries in North Africa.
   a.

   b.

   c.

5. List three countries in East Africa.
   a.

   b.

   c.

6. List three countries in West Africa.
   a.

   b.

   c.

7. List three countries in Central Africa.
   a.

   b.

   c.

8. List three countries in Southern Africa.
   a.

   b.

   c.

Name:_____

Africa in the Late Nineteenth Century

Instructions: Use the map to answer the questions that follow.

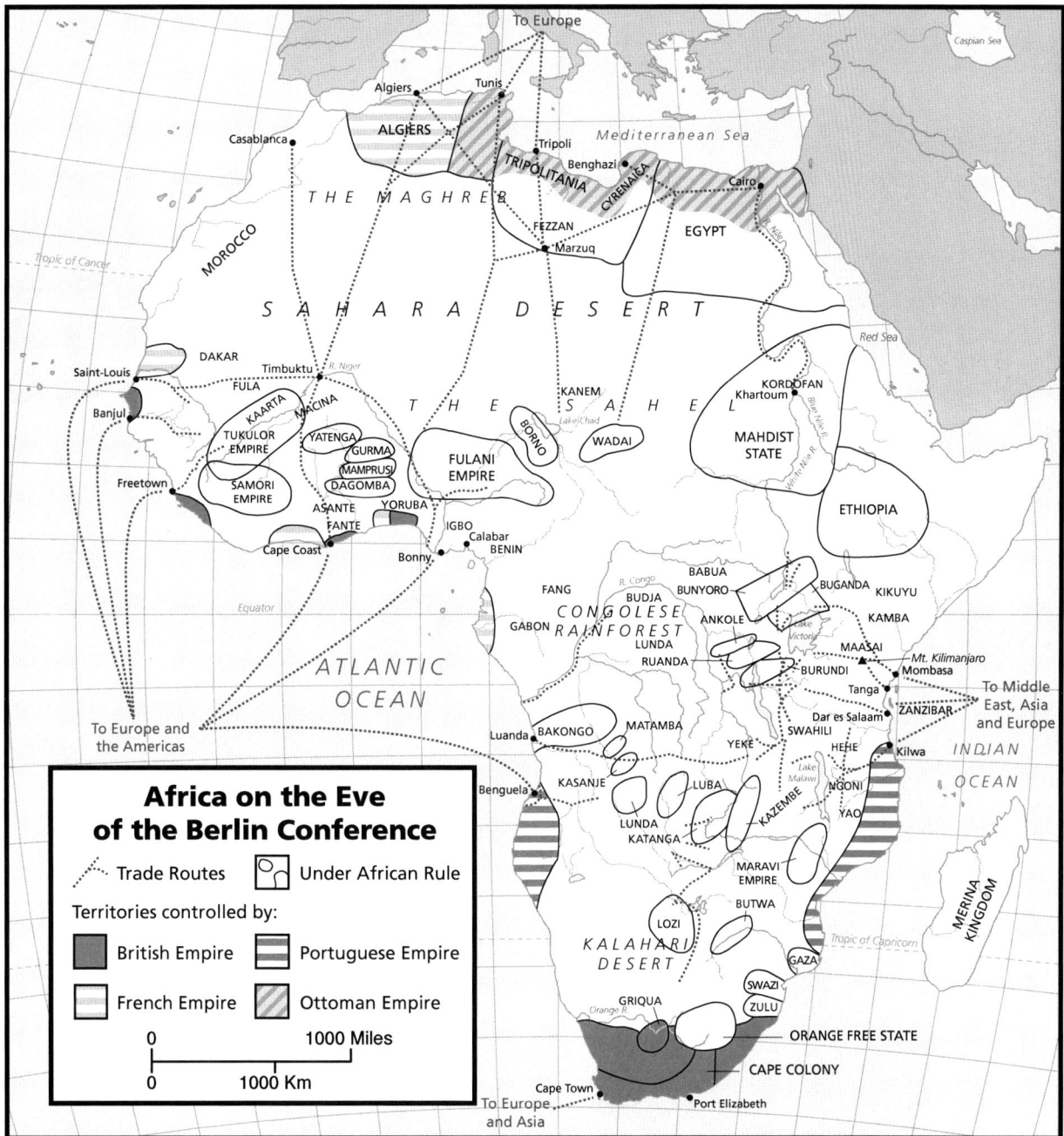

Questions:
1. a. Which regions of Africa conducted international trade? (Hint: use the regions referred to on the map "Africa Today.")

TRB 12 | Colonization and Independence in Africa
Day One

Name:_____

  b. Which regions of the world did Africans trade with?

2. To which continents was Timbuktu connected by trade?

3. List five coastal cities that conducted international trade. If any of these cities were controlled by an empire include it in parentheses. For example, *Cape Town (British Empire)*.

   a.   d.

   b.   e.

   c.

4. List four major African empires, kingdoms, or societies and describe where they are located. For example, *Tukulor Empire, West Africa*.

   a.   c.

   b.   d.

5. What parts of the continent did Europeans claim? Using this map, make a general statement about the location of European territories in Africa in the nineteenth century.

Name:_____

Colonization and Independence in Africa
Day One
TRB
13

Africa in 1914

Instructions: Use the map to answer the questions that follow.

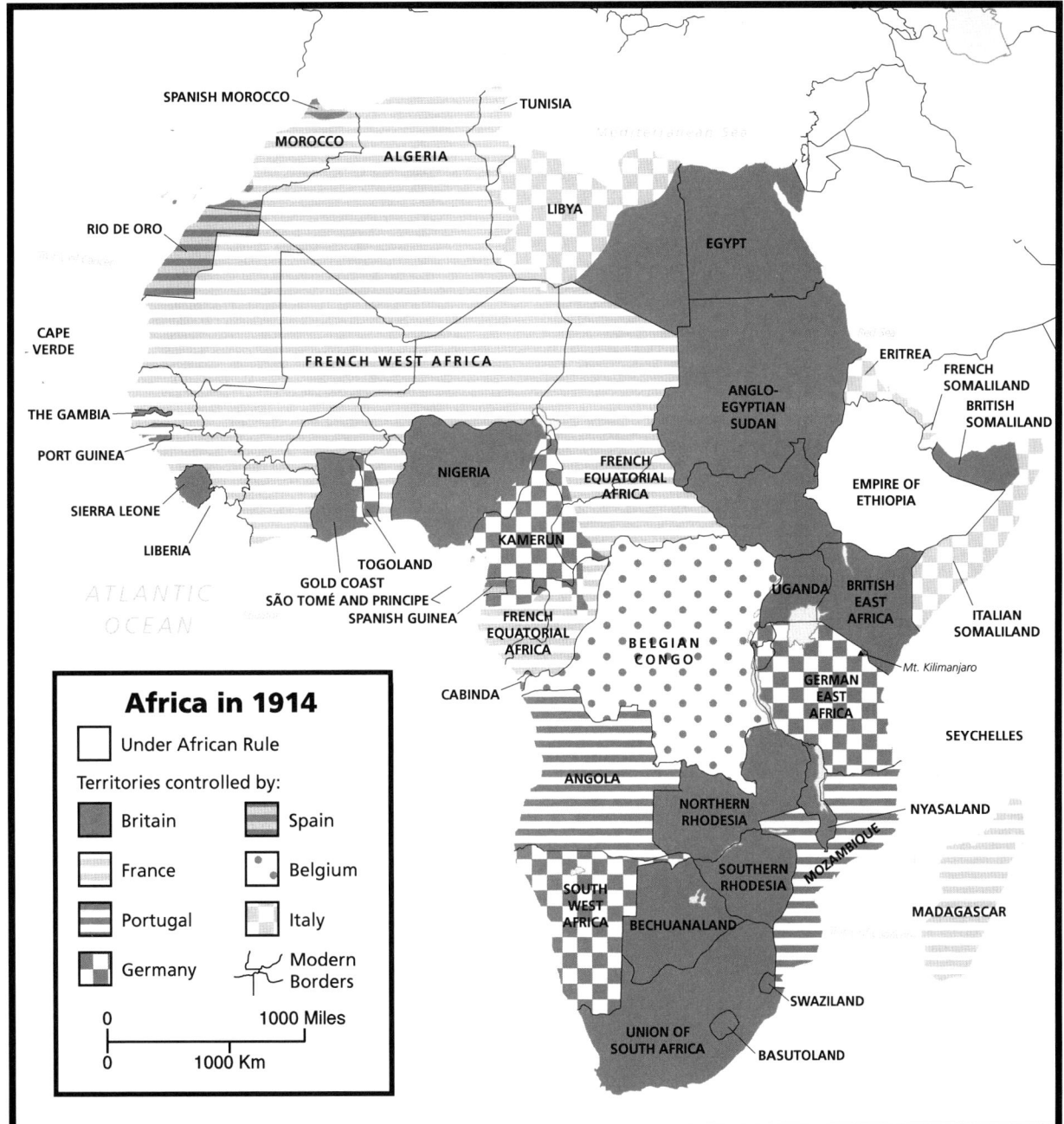

Questions:
1. Which European countries controlled territory in Africa?

Colonization and Independence in Africa
Day One

Name:_____

2. Which two European countries claimed the most territory?

3. Which African countries were independent in 1914? (Hint: Look for regions under African rule.)

4. Using the reading and your knowledge of history, what major world event began in 1914? How did the end of this event change the map of colonial Africa?

5. Compare the map of 1914 with the map of the late nineteenth century. Find two African empires or societies that were split between more than one colony by 1914. Find two African empires or societies that were contained within a single colony in 1914. (You may find it helpful to draw the boundaries of African societies onto the 1914 map.)

   a. Empires split between colonies:

   b. Empires contained within a single colony:

6. Estimate how much of the African continent Europe claimed prior to 1880 (nineteenth-century map). (For example, 10 percent, 50 percent, 90 percent, etc.)

7. Estimate how much of Africa fell under European rule by 1914.

8. Compare the map of 1914 with the map of Africa today. How do you think the boundaries of colonial territories shaped the boundaries of countries on the continent today?

Source Analysis: Different Perspectives on a Violent Encounter

Objectives:
Students will: Analyze primary sources that present different perspectives on the same event.

Assess the value of first-hand accounts for historical understanding of nineteenth-century Africa.

Consider the value of multiple sources for understanding history.

Required Reading:
Students should have read Part I of the student text and completed "Study Guide—Introduction and Part I" (TRB 5-6) or "Advanced Study Guide—Introduction and Part I" (TRB-7).

Handouts:
"Violence along the Congo River in 1877" (TRB 16-17)

"Source Analysis" (TRB 18-19)

In the Classroom:
1. Focus Question—Put the question "How do we know what is true?" on the board. Brainstorm answers for a few minutes as a class and record noteworthy points. You may want to review concepts such as evidence, fact, opinion, and bias.

2. Group Work—Divide students into small groups or pairs and distribute the handouts "Violence along the Congo River in 1877" and "Source Analysis." Tell students to follow the directions carefully and complete the questions.

3. Making Connections—After students have completed the handouts, have everyone come together in a large group. Ask students to share their findings.

Challenge students to summarize what events and descriptions are consistent between the two sources. Have students summarize what events or descriptions differ between the two sources. Make a list of students' answers on the board.

How reliable do students think these sources are? What is the benefit of reading both sources? Do students feel as though they can describe what happened during this encounter based on these two sources?

What impressions would someone in nineteenth century Europe have of Africa if they only read Stanley's account? Why might this be significant?

What questions do these sources raise about early encounters between Africans and outsiders? What other sources or information would students want to have to answer these questions?

4. Ethics and Knowledge—Ask students what they might say if a student or teacher from another class gave a presentation based solely on Stanley's account of these events. What are the arguments for considering Chief Mojimba's account? How does considering a single perspective affect our understanding of history?

Homework:
Students should read Part II of the student text and complete "Study Guide—Part II" (TRB 22-23) or "Advanced Study Guide—Part II" (TRB-24).

Violence along the Congo River in 1877

Instructions: In this activity, you will read two primary sources—one by an American journalist and adventurer and the other by an African chief—that describe a violent encounter in 1877 between the authors along part of the Congo River (present-day Zaire). Read the sources carefully. Using different colors, mark statements that are presented as facts and those that are opinion. Then answer the questions. Be prepared to share your answers with the class.

■ Source 1: Henry Morton Stanley

Henry Morton Stanley, a Welsh-born American journalist and adventurer, was instrumental in developing treaties to give King Leopold II of Belgium control of the Congo River region. In the account below, Stanley describes his experiences while travelling by canoe along the Congo River in 1877 with a number of companions.

About 8AM we came in view of a marketplace, near which there were scores of small canoes. The men at once rushed into them and advanced all round us. We refrained a long time, but finally, as they became emboldened by our stillness and began to launch their wooden spears, which they proceeded to do all together…we were obliged to reply to them with a few shots, which compelled them to scamper away ahead of us. Drums then awakened the whole country, and horns blew deafening blasts….

We came, about 10AM, to another market green. Here, too, warriors were ready, and again we had to recourse to our weapons. The little canoes with loud threats disappeared quickly down river: the land warriors rushed away into the woods….

At 2PM we emerged out of the shelter of the deeply wooded banks and came into a vast stream nearly 2,000 yards across at the mouth…. We pulled briskly over to gain the right bank when, looking upstream, we saw a sight that sent the blood tingling through every nerve and fiber of our bodies: a flotilla of gigantic canoes bearing down upon us, which both in size and numbers greatly exceeded anything we had seen hitherto!...

We had sufficient time to take a view of the mighty force bearing down on us and to count the number of the war vessels. There were 54 four of them! A monster canoe led the way with two rows of upstanding paddles, 40 men on a side, their bodies bending and swaying in unison as with a swelling barbarous chorus they drove her down toward us….

The crashing sound of large drums, a hundred blasts from ivory horns, and a thrilling chant from 2,000 human throats did not tend to soothe our nerves or to increase our confidence. However it was "neck or nothing." We had no time to pray or to take sentimental looks at the savage world, or even to breathe a sad farewell to it….

As the foremost canoe came rushing down, its consorts on either side beating the water into foam and raising their jets of water with their sharp prows, I turned to take a last look at our people and said to them:

"Boys, be firm as iron; wait until you see the first spear and then take good aim. Don't fire all at once. Keep aiming until you are sure of your man. Don't think of running away, for only your guns can save you."

The monster canoe aimed straight for my boat, as though it would run us down; but when within fifty yards off, it swerved aside and, when nearly opposite, the warriors above the manned prow let fly their spears and on either side there was a noise of rushing bodies. But every sound was soon lost in the ripping, crackling musketry. For five minutes we were so absorbed in firing that we took no note of anything else; but at the end of that time we were made aware that the enemy was reforming about 200 yards above us.

Our blood was up now. It was a murderous world, and we felt for the first time that we hated the filthy, vulturous ghouls who inhabited it. We therefore lifted our anchors and pursued them upstream along the right bank until, rounding a point, we saw their villages. We made straight for the banks and continued the fight in the village streets with those who had landed, hunting them out into the woods, and there only sounded the retreat, having returned the daring cannibals the compliment of a visit.

* Adapted from Henry Stanley, *Through the Dark Continent*, Vol. II. (New York: Harper & Row, 1885).

■ Source 2: Chief Mojimba

Chief Mojimba, an African leader in the Congo River region, led the greeting party that met Stanley and his companions on the river. Mojimba told his story of the encounter with Stanley years later to a Catholic missionary, Father Joseph Fraessle. Fraessle published Mojimba's account decades later.

When we heard that the man with the white flesh was journeying down the Lualaba (Lualaba-Congo) we were open-mouthed with astonishment. We stood still. All night long the drums announced the strange news—a man with white flesh! That man, we said to ourselves, has a white skin. He must have got that from the river-kingdom. He will be one of our brothers who were drowned in the river. All life comes from the water, and in the water he has found life. Now is coming back to us, he is coming home....

We will prepare a feast, I ordered, we will go to meet our brother and escort him into the village with rejoicing! We donned our ceremonial garb. We assembled the great canoes. We listened for the gong which would announce our brother's presence on the Lualaba. Presently the cry was heard: He is approaching the Lohali! Now he enters the river! Halloh! We swept forward, my canoe leading, the others following, with songs of joy and with dancing, to meet the first white man our eyes had beheld, and to do him honor.

But as we drew near his canoes there were loud reports, bang! Bang! And fire-staves spat bits of iron at us. We were paralyzed with fright; our mouths hung wide open and we could not shut them. Things such as we had never seen, never heard of, never dreamed of—they were the work of evil spirits! Several of my men plunged into the water.... What for? Did they fly to safety? No—for others fell down also, in the canoes. Some screamed dreadfully, others were silent—they were dead, and blood flowed from little holes in their bodies. "War! that is war!" I yelled. "Go back!" The canoes sped back to our village with all the strength our spirits could impart to our arms.

That was no brother! That was the worst enemy our country had ever seen.

And still those bangs went on; the long staves spat fire, flying pieces of iron whistled around us, fell into the water with a hissing sound, and our brothers continued to fall. We fled into our village—they came after us. We fled into the forest and flung ourselves on the ground. When we returned that evening our eyes beheld fearful things: our brothers, dead, bleeding, our village plundered and burned, and the water full of dead bodies.

* Adapted from Heinrich Schiffers, *The Quest for Africa—Two Thousand Years of Exploration* (New York: G.P. Putnam's Sons, 1957).

TRB 18 | Colonization and Independence in Africa
Optional Lesson

Name:_____

Source Analysis

Instructions: Now that you have read the two sources and marked statements that are fact or opinion, answer the set of questions below. Be prepared to share your answers with the class.

Questions

1. a. When and where did Stanley and Chief Mojimba's encounter take place?

   b. When were these sources published and by whom?
   Source 1:

   Source 2:

2. List three facts that the sources agree on.
   a.

   b.

   c.

3. What are two important pieces of information mentioned in one account and not the other?

   Stanley's account:
   a.

   b.

   Chief Mojimba's account:
   a.

   b.

■ The Choices Program ■ Watson Institute for International Studies, Brown University ■ www.choices.edu

Name:_____

4. How do Stanley and Chief Mojimba describe each other? Provide specific examples. What does this tell us about them?

5. How does each account describe the use of violence?

   Stanley:

   Chief Mojimba:

6. Is Stanley's account biased in any way? Explain.

7. Is Chief Mojimba's account biased in any way? Explain.

8. If a historian were studying early encounters between Africans and Europeans, what could they learn by studying these sources?

Photo Analysis: Look Again

Objectives:

Students will: Analyze a photographic source.

Consider the benefits and limitations of using photographs for understanding history.

Review the role of missionaries in the colonization and documentation of African societies.

Required Reading:

Before beginning the lesson, students should have read Part II of the student text and completed "Study Guide—Part II" (TRB 22-23) or "Advanced Study Guide—Part II" (TRB-24).

Handouts:

"Photo Analysis: Pastor Koranteng" (TRB 26-27)

"Look Again: Akua Oye" (TRB-28)

Resources:

You will find a PowerPoint of the image online at <www.choices.edu/colonizationmaterials>.

An in-depth video analysis of the postcard featured in this lesson by historian and archivist Paul Jenkins can be found at <http://vimeo.com/33251261>. The video should be viewed by students only after they have completed the whole activity.

In the Classroom:

1. The Role of Missionaries—Tell students that they will be analyzing a photograph on a postcard produced by a Christian mission working in the Gold Coast. These postcards were sometimes used by missionaries to communicate with relatives and friends back home, but they were mostly sent for publicity and to gain financial support for their work abroad. Mission postcards were often sent to churches and Christian homes in Europe and the United States.

2. Examining a Missionary Postcard—Divide the class into small groups of three to four and distribute the first handout, "Photo Analysis: Pastor Koranteng." Review the instructions with students and have them answer the questions. (Students may need a hint about the European practice of reversing the month and day in the date on the photo.) After ten minutes, have students share their observations.

Now distribute the second handout, "Look Again: Akua Oye," and have students read the new information about the photograph and answer the questions in their groups. You might also choose to review this new information together with the whole class.

3. Reconsidering the Past—How did the information provided on the second handout change students' understanding of the photograph? Why do students think Rudolph Fisch's caption emphasized the pastor instead of Akua Oye? With this new information, what other questions about the photograph, the photographer, or the family do students have?

Have some students share their alternative captions for the photo.

4. Becoming a More Thorough Historian—Ask students to consider the difference between their answers to the questions on the first worksheet, "Photo Analysis: Pastor Koranteng," and the second worksheet, "Look Again: Akua Oye." What contributed to their initial understanding of the source? How does this relate to the purpose of the photographer Rudolf Fisch? Did Fisch influence their interpretation? Why did their perspective change? What are the benefits and limitations of using materials produced by missionaries as a resource for learning about colonization in Africa?

How might the lessons students learned from examining this photograph apply to examining other visual sources?

5. Extra Challenge: Brainstorm a list of guidelines and standard questions for examining photographic sources. Here is a list of possible questions:

- Who and what is in the photograph?
- What is happening in the photo?
- Is there any reason to believe or suggest that the photograph has been altered?
- Would looking at other sources help to explain what is shown?
- Who took it and why?
- Were the people in the photo posing for the photographer or were they unaware that the picture was taken?
- Is there a caption or title?
- Is the photo a selective or misleading view of an event?
- What ideas or biases do we have that might affect how we interpret the photo?

There are thousands of missionary postcards available online at the International Mission Photography Archive, <http://digitallibrary.usc.edu/cdm/landingpage/collection/p15799coll123>. Have students use their new list of standard questions for photographic sources to analyze any of these images. You may want to remind them that not all sources contain dramatic discoveries or hidden meanings.

Study Guide—Part II

Vocabulary: Be sure that you understand these key terms from Part II of your reading. Circle ones that you do not know.

anticolonial
nationalism
migrated
traditional leaders
blockade
conscripted

subsistence farming
fascism
self-determination
United Nations
the Cold War
authoritarian

Questions:

1. List two ways educated Africans helped organize resistance efforts in cities.
    a.

    b.

2. Define "mandate," as it was used by the League of Nations.

3. What was the...
    a. Pan African Congress?

    b. Universal Negro Improvement Association?

4. List three ways Africans opposed colonialism following World War I.
    a.

    b.

    c.

5. Why was nationalist unity difficult to achieve in some regions of Africa?

6. How did Italy's invasion of Ethiopia influence African nationalist perspectives about colonialism?

7. How did the following groups interpret the United Nations founding goal: "equal rights and [the] self-determination of peoples"?

   a. Nationalist groups in Africa:

   b. European colonial powers:

8. Why did Britain and France intensify their efforts to control colonial economies after World War II?

9. How did the emergence of mass political parties change the nature of African demands for independence?

Advanced Study Guide—Part II

1. What impact did the end of World War I have on African colonies under European rule?

2. What role did Pan Africanism play in the growth of anticolonial nationalism?

3. What methods did anticolonial groups in Africa use to resist colonial rule during the 1920s and 1930s?

4. How did world opinion on colonization shift after World War II?

Part II Graphic Organizer

Name: _____

Pan-African Movement
What was the Pan-African movement?

When did it start?

When did it gain momentum?

Invasion of Ethiopia: _____ (year)
Who invaded Ethiopia?

What was Europe's response?

What did this response signal to African nationalist groups?

World War I
How were African colonies involved in the war effort?

African Political Parties
What groups joined African political parties following World War II?

What did many African political parties call for?

World War II
How were African colonies involved in the war effort?

African Resistance
List some of the ways Africans resisted colonialism.
-
-
-

End of World War II
Which countries still had colonies in Africa following the war?

How did world opinion on colonialism begin to shift?

Photo Analysis: Pastor Koranteng

Instructions: Examine the photograph and answer the questions that follow. The photograph's caption was written by the photographer, Rudolph Fisch, a Swiss Protestant missionary in the Gold Coast. Remember that historians often use photographs to gain an impression about an event or era. Nevertheless, it is important to be careful about drawing conclusions from photographs. One cannot be certain that a photograph is an accurate or complete reflection of reality.

"The African Pastor Koranteng and His Family." Photo by Rudolph Fisch.

1. Who and what do you see? (Provide at least five details about the photograph.)

Name:_____

2. When and where was this photograph taken?

3. a. Who took the photograph?

   b. What do we know about the photographer?

4. What does the caption tell you about the photograph?

5. Does the photograph have a point of view? Explain.

6. What do you think the purpose of the photograph is?

Look Again: Akua Oye

Instructions: You have already recorded your impressions about the photo based on your initial observations. In this part of the activity, you will reconsider your impressions based on new information about the photo. The information comes from Paul Jenkins, a historian who studied this photo and the role of missionaries in colonial Africa.

New Information

❖ Missionaries referred to the pastor's wife as Mrs. Amelia Koranteng. This was the name they had given her. But she was known to members of her own community as *ohemmaa*, or "queen mother." She was the most important female in the Akwapin Kingdom (a region of present-day Ghana). Her name was Akua Oye.

❖ As "queen mother," Akua Oye did not hold the highest political title in the Akwapin Kingdom. This role was reserved for the king, but his right to rule the kingdom had to be authorized by the "queen mother." The "queen mother" was not married to the king, but she chose the king from many candidates, including her nephews, her own children, and other male relatives.

❖ The location of Akua Oye in the center of the photo and the grouping of the female children around her, and not around Pastor Koranteng, suggests her central importance in her family and community.

❖ Except for Pastor Koranteng, the photograph only features female relatives of Akua Oye. This is probably not a coincidence because the Akwapin Kingdom was a matrilineal society (all heirs are traced through the mother and maternal ancestors).

❖ Akua Oye is sitting in the center of the photograph, wearing African clothing. Meanwhile, the pastor, the children, and the young woman are wearing European-style clothing and are standing or sitting to her side. In other missionary photographs of African pastors and their families, usually all members of the family are dressed in European-style clothing.

Questions

1. List three discoveries from the new information above that you find the most interesting or important.

2. Why do you think Rudolph Fisch's caption did not contain information about Akua Oye?

3. Write an alternative, and more accurate, caption for the photograph.

Kikuyu Fable: A Tale of Resistance

Objectives:
Students will: Analyze a Kikuyu fable describing colonialism in Kenya.

Collaborate in groups to create a dramatic or artistic interpretation of the story.

Required Reading:
Before beginning the lesson, students should have read Part II of the student text and completed "Study Guide—Part II" (TRB 22-23) or "Advanced Study Guide—Part II" (TRB-24).

Handouts:
"The Man and the Elephant" (TRB 30-31)

Note: It may take two class periods to complete the lesson. For a shorter lesson, refer to parts 1 and 2, and conclude with part 4.

In the Classroom:
1. Reflecting on Liberation Movements— Have students think back on what they read in Part II. Why did many Africans have grievances against the colonial system? Why did African nationalist movements grow in popularity after World War II?

2. Group Work— Divide students into small groups of three to four students. Give each group copies of the handout. Tell students that they will be reading a story that was told by the Kikuyu during the colonial period. (The Kikuyu were the largest ethnic group in Kenya, and many Kikuyu were involved in the Mau Mau conflict in the 1950s.) Students should carefully read the directions and work with their group members to answer the questions.

3. Sharing the Story— While remaining in groups, review the handout with the class. What did the man, the hut, and the animals represent? From whose perspective was this story written? What is the overall message?

Now tell students that their groups will create an artistic representation of the story. Groups may wish to create:

    a. a cartoon strip, or political cartoon.

    b. a dramatic reenactment of the story.

    c. a political pamphlet or poster.

Once students have completed their preparations, have groups present to the class.

4. Culminating Discussion— Ask students to make connections between the ideas in this story and what they know about African resistance and struggles for independence.

Why is there a conflict between the man and the animals? How did the man try to resolve this conflict? How does the Commission of Inquiry justify the animals' occupation of the man's hut? Why is he eventually driven to violence? How are these ideas related to what students know about African independence struggles?

Ask students to consider the effect that this story might have had. If you were a Kikuyu in colonial Kenya in the 1930s, how would hearing this story make you feel? What would be the benefit of conveying this message in a story, as opposed to a political pamphlet or newspaper article? How could a story like this be a form of resistance? Why do students think that resistance of this type was so important?

The Man and the Elephant

Instructions: The following Kikuyu story (originally told in the Kikuyu language) describes relations between the Kikuyu and Europeans in Kenya. (The Kikuyu were the largest ethnic group in Kenya, and many Kikuyu were involved in the Mau Mau conflict in the 1950s.) This story was first published in 1938 in a book by Jomo Kenyatta, who would eventually become the first president of Kenya. Kenyans won their independence from Britain in 1962. The following version of this story was told by Ndabaningi Sithole, a Zimbabwean reverend and political leader.

An elephant made friendship with a man. Driven by a heavy thunderstorm, the elephant sought shelter in the man's hut that was on the edge of the forest. The elephant was allowed partial admission, but eventually he evicted the man from his hut and took full possession of the hut, saying: "My dear good friend, your skin is harder than mine, and there is not enough room for both of us. You can afford to remain in the rain while I am protecting my delicate skin from the hailstorm."

A dispute between the elephant and the man ensued. This attracted the notice of the King of the Jungle. In the interest of peace and good order the Lion assured the grumbling man that he would appoint a Commission of Inquiry: "You have done well by establishing a friendship with my people, especially with the elephant, who is one of my honorable ministers of state. Do not grumble anymore, your hut is not lost to you. Wait until the sitting of my Imperial Commission, and there you will be given plenty of opportunity to state your case. I am sure you will be pleased with the findings of the Commission."

The Commission was duly appointed. It comprised (1) Mr. Rhinoceros; (2) Mr. Buffalo; (3) Mr. Alligator; (4) The Rt. Hon. Mr. Fox to act as chairman; and (5) Mr. Leopard to act as Secretary to the Commission. The man asked that one of his kind be included on the Commission, but he was assured that none of his kind was educated enough to understand the intricacy of jungle law, and that the members of the Commission were God-chosen and would execute their business with justice.

The elephant gave his evidence: "Gentleman of the Jungle, there is no need for me to waste your valuable time in relating a story which I am sure you all know. I have always regarded it as my duty to protect the interests of my friends, and this appears to have caused the misunderstanding between myself and my friend here. He invited me to save his hut from being blown away by a hurricane. As the hurricane had gained access owing [to] the unoccupied space in the hut, I considered it necessary, in my friend's own interests, to turn the undeveloped space to a more economic use by sitting in it myself; a duty which any of you would undoubtedly have performed with equal readiness in similar circumstances."

Next the man gave interrupted evidence and the Commission delivered its verdict as follows: "In our opinion this dispute has arisen through a regrettable misunderstanding due to the backwardness of your ideas. We consider that Mr. Elephant has fulfilled his sacred duty of protecting your interest. As it is clearly for your good that the space should be put to its economic use, and as you yourself have not yet reached the age of expansion which would enable you to fill it, we consider it necessary to arrange a compromise to suit both parties. Mr. Elephant shall continue his occupation of your hut, but we give you permission to look for a site where you can build another hut more suited to your needs, and we shall see that you are well protected."

The man, fearing exposure to the teeth and claws of the members of the Commission, had no alternative. He built another hut. Mr. Rhinoceros came and occupied it. Another Commission of Inquiry was set up. The man was advised to look for a new site. This went on until all the members of the Commission had been properly housed at the expense of the man. Then the desperate man said to himself, "Ng'enda thi ndeagaga motegi" (There is nothing that treads on the earth that cannot be trapped; i.e., You can fool people for a time, but not forever).

So the man built a big hut, and soon the lords of the jungle came and occupied the big hut. The man shut them in and set the hut on fire and all perished. The man returned home, saying: "Peace is costly, but it's worth the expense."

Questions

1. Summarize this story in three to four sentences.

2. In the story, the man, the hut, and the animals are symbols that represent something else. What do these symbols stand for?

    a. the man:

    b. the hut:

    c. the animals:

3. Whose perspective is represented in this story?

4. Why do you think the Kikuyu told this story? Who was their audience?

5. What is the message of this story?

The Four Case Studies: Organization and Preparation

Objectives:
Students will: Analyze differences between African and European perspectives on colonization.

Identify the core assumptions underlying each perspective.

Work cooperatively within groups to organize effective visual presentations.

Required Reading:
Students should have read "Case Studies" and "Case Studies in Brief" in the student text.

Handouts:
"Presenting Your Case Study" (TRB-33)

"Case Studies: Graphic Organizer" (TRB-34)

In the Classroom:
1. Planning for Group Work—In order to save time in the classroom, form student groups before beginning Day Three. During the class period, students will be preparing their presentations. Remind them to use information from the reading to support their presentations.

2. Case Study Groups—Divide the class into four groups. Assign a case study to each group. Each case study has a central question that is explored in the reading and primary sources.

Inform students that each group is responsible for creating a political cartoon. These cartoons should illustrate the differences between African and European views about the central question of their case study. Each group will present their political cartoon as well as a summary of their assigned case study and central question to the class. Groups should follow the instructions in "Presenting Your Case Study." Groups should begin by assigning each member a role (students may double up).

3. Evaluating the Case Studies—Give each student a copy of "Case Studies: Graphic Organizer." Students should fill in the row that corresponds to their assigned case study while they are preparing their presentations. During class presentations, they should fill in the remainder of the chart.

Homework:
Students should complete preparations for the presentation.

Name:_____

Presenting Your Case Study

Your Assignment: Your group has been assigned a colonization case study. Your assignment is to explain the case study to your classmates, both in a 4-5 minute presentation and in a political cartoon. The cartoon should represent how Europeans and Africans held different views on colonization. As you consider these perspectives, start with how some Europeans and Africans answered the central question of your assigned case study.

Organizing Your Group: Each member of your group will take on a specific role. Below is a brief explanation of the responsibility of each role. Before preparing your sections of the presentation, work together to address the questions below. The **group director** is responsible for organizing your presentation. The **historian** is responsible for providing an overview of your assigned country and an explanation of the central question. The **European perspective expert** is responsible for explaining European views on the central question. The **African perspective expert** is responsible for explaining African views on the central question. The **cartoonist** is responsible for presenting your group's political cartoon.

Questions to Consider

1. a. What is your assigned country?

   b. What is the colonizing power?

2. What is the central question of your assigned case?

3. How did the colonizing power govern your assigned country?

4. What were the African experiences of colonialism in your assigned country?

Colonization and Independence in Africa
Graphic Organizer

TRB 34

Name:_____

Case Studies: Graphic Organizer

Instructions: As you prepare your presentation, fill in the row that corresponds to your assigned case study. During the presentations of other case study groups, fill in the remainder of the chart.

	Colonizing Power	Years under Colonial Rule	Central Question	How did (some) Africans answer this question?	How did (some) Europeans answer this question?
Ghana					
Democratic Republic of the Congo					
Algeria					
Kenya					

The Four Case Studies: Presentation and Discussion

Objectives:

Students will: Articulate the perspectives of African and European groups.

Cooperate with classmates in staging a presentation.

Consider how different perspectives inform our understanding of colonization.

In the Classroom:

1. Setting the Stage—Tell students that they will be historians presenting and listening to the perspectives of groups within four colonies. Each of these cases has a central question that was an important element of the colonial experiences of that country. As they listen to the presentations, students should consider how the issues raised by each central question affected colonial policies, African experiences of colonialism, and African resistance to colonialism.

2. Managing the Presentations—Be sure that each student has their copy of "Case Studies: Graphic Organizer." Explain that each group will give a four-to-five minute presentation to the class explaining the case that they have been assigned, describing the central question, and presenting their political cartoon. As groups present, the rest of the class should fill in the graphic organizer. When each group finishes its presentation, allow students to ask any questions they may have.

3. Guiding Discussion—Have students consider the information on their graphic organizer. In what ways were European and African views fundamentally different with regard to these contested issues? Why do students think their views were so different? Do students think particular perspectives are more valid or accurate than others? Why?

At the time, which groups had the power to express their views to a wide audience? What audiences could they reach, and how? What are some possible consequences of this? For example, how might the views of people in Britain or France have been affected by their limited access to African perspectives? Why might this be important?

What views are missing from this discussion? For example, how might the opinions of a Kikuyu woman, an unemployed youth in the Belgian Congo, or an elderly Algerian man who does not speak French differ from the views that are presented? Encourage students to be as specific as possible. How might these views help us better understand these topics and this time period?

Homework:

Students should read the Epilogue in the student text and complete the "Study Guide—Epilogue" (TRB 37-38) or the "Advanced Study Guide—Epilogue" (TRB-39).

The All-African People's Conference, Accra, Ghana, 1958

Objectives:
Students will: Consider the historical events surrounding the 1958 All-African People's Conference.

Assess a primary source document.

Analyze, synthesize, and present data about the independence of African states.

Work collaboratively with classmates.

Required Reading:
Before beginning the lesson, students should have read "Epilogue: African Independence" in the student text and completed "Study Guide—Epilogue" (TRB 37-38) or "Advanced Study Guide—Epilogue" (TRB-39).

Handouts:
"The All-African People's Conference" (TRB-41)

"Resolution on Imperialism and Colonialism" (TRB 42-44)

"African Independence in the Twentieth Century" (TRB 45-46)

"Charting African Independence" (TRB-47)

Note: Students may find colored pencils for the timeline and graphing activity helpful. Students might also find the map "Africa Today" (TRB-9) useful.

In the Classroom:
1. Setting the Stage—Ask students to recall their readings. What were the primary reasons that Africans wanted independence? Distribute "The All-African People's Conference" and review its main points with the class.

2. Working in Groups—Divide the class into groups of three to four students and distribute the remaining handouts to each group. Groups should work through and discuss the questions and activities. Students should record their group's responses on their own worksheets.

Some students might need coaching about making the graph. Emphasize the importance of labeling the graph clearly.

3. Sharing Conclusions and Discussion—Ask groups to share their findings and compare answers with the other groups. What did delegates condemn in the "Resolution on Imperialism and Colonialism"? What were the primary aspirations and demands? Which of the aspirations or demands do students find particularly interesting or surprising? Why?

Have students examine their graphs. How many African countries were independent in 1958? In what year did the most countries achieve independence?

Have students recall their reading. Why was Africa undergoing political change at the time of the All-African People's Conference? What were some of the challenges that newly independent countries faced? What caused these challenges? Do students believe that the period of rapid independence of African countries is a major historical event? Why or why not?

4. Extra Challenge: Have students do a short research project on one of the African countries that achieved independence other than the four case studies covered in the reading. When was the country colonized and by what country? What were the European colonial interests in the colony? What were the primary issues during the colonial period? What were the circumstances of its independence? What were the major political, social, and economic developments after independence?

Name:_____

Study Guide—Epilogue

Vocabulary: Be sure that you understand these key terms from the Epilogue of your reading. Circle ones that you do not know.

legacies
elites
international relations

majority rule
apartheid
Non-Aligned Movement

Questions:

1. Why did France treat Algeria differently than its colonies in West and Central Africa?

2. List two ways that Britain and France tried to preserve their interests in former colonies.

    a.

    b.

3. What other regions of the world were undergoing decolonization at the same time African states were becoming independent?

4. a. What two superpowers emerged after World War II?

    b. In what ways were these superpowers involved in the Congo after it gained independence from Belgium?

TRB 38 | Colonization and Independence in Africa
Day Five

Name:_____

5. What was the mission of the Non-Aligned Movement?

6. How did colonial education policies affect the capabilities of newly independent African states to govern and develop their economies?

7. List four new industries developed in African countries following independence.
   a.   c.

   b.   d.

8. What event marked the end of colonial rule in Africa?

9. For decades after _____, African scholars, _____, and _____ worked to counter the psychological effects of colonialism, and to rekindle _____ in African_____ and _____.

10. What role does the African Union play?

Name:_____

Colonization and Independence in Africa
Day Five

TRB **39**

Advanced Study Guide—Epilogue

1. In what ways did Britain and France try to influence their former colonies after independence?

2. How did the Cold War struggle between the United States and the Soviet Union affect certain countries in Africa?

3. How did political and economic challenges affect newly independent African countries?

4. How do the legacies of colonialism affect Africa today?

African Independence

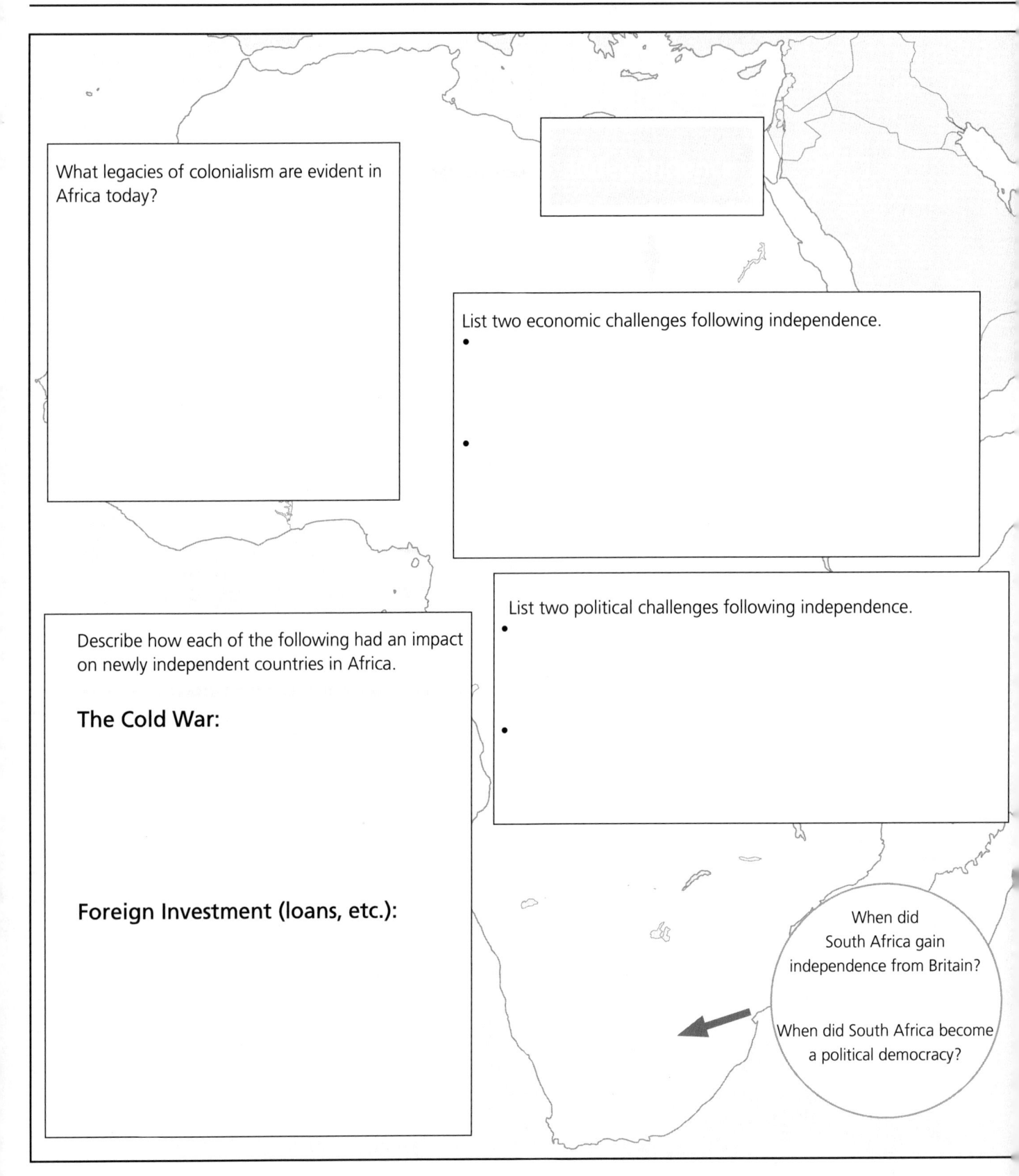

What legacies of colonialism are evident in Africa today?

List two economic challenges following independence.
-
-

List two political challenges following independence.
-
-

Describe how each of the following had an impact on newly independent countries in Africa.

The Cold War:

Foreign Investment (loans, etc.):

When did South Africa gain independence from Britain?

When did South Africa become a political democracy?

The All-African People's Conference

In December 1958, over three hundred delegates from twenty-eight African countries gathered in Accra, Ghana to participate in the All-African People's Conference. The delegates in attendance were anticolonial nationalist leaders, representatives from political parties, members of labor organizations, and freedom fighters who were working tirelessly to liberate their countries from colonialism. Other delegates came from independent African countries, many of which had only recently achieved an end to colonial rule. The independent countries represented at the conference were Egypt, Eritrea, Ethiopia, Ghana, Guinea, Liberia, Libya, Morocco, and Tunisia.*

The All-African People's Conference took place during a critical moment in history. Ghana, the host country, had achieved independence just a year earlier in 1957. Reflecting on the end of colonial rule in his country, the Ghanaian Prime Minister Kwame Nkrumah announced, "The independence of Ghana is meaningless unless it is linked to the total liberation of the African continent." This message reassured others fighting for liberation that they would not be alone in their struggles. The fact that the delegates gathered in Accra, the capital of Ghana, added a sense of triumph to the conference. Slogans such as "Hands Off Africa! Africa Must be Free!" and "Down with Imperialism and Colonialism" draped the walls of the conference room. These slogans reflected delegates' commitment to liberating not just their own countries from colonial rule, but also the entire African continent.

A wide range of topics were discussed, including strategies to speed up the process of liberation, the value of nonviolent versus violent resistance, and the idea of creating a "United States of Africa." The idea of a united Africa received both strong support and strong opposition. While a united Africa failed to gain enough support, other ideas were put into action. For example, a "Freedom Fund" was established to provide financial backing to liberation movements across the continent. A document titled "Resolution on Imperialism and Colonialism" also came out of the conference. It drew on the theme of universal human rights and demanded that these be extended to all Africans. The delegates emphasized the importance of this goal with their decision to establish a permanent committee to investigate human rights abuses across Africa.

*Sudan achieved independence in 1956, but did not have a delegation at the conference.

Resolution on Imperialism and Colonialism

Instructions: The first part of the resolution expresses what the delegates condemn about imperialism and colonialism. As you read, use different colors to mark 1) words or phrases that you do not understand; and 2) key terms or phrases that show what the delegates opposed (for example, "economic exploitation").

The second part of the resolution expresses the delegates' aspirations and demands. As you read, use different colors to mark 1) words or phrases that you do not understand; and 2) key terms or phrases that show what the delegates want for the future of Africa (for example, "a human rights committee"). Then answer the questions that follow.

Note: "Franchise" means the right to vote.

All-African People's Conference: Resolution on Imperialism and Colonialism, Accra, December 5-13, 1958

(1) Whereas the great bulk of the African continent has been carved out arbitrarily to the detriment of the indigenous African peoples by European Imperialists, namely: Britain, France, Belgium, Spain, Italy and Portugal.

(2) Whereas in this process of colonisation, two groups of colonial territories have emerged...:

(a) Those territories where indigenous Africans are dominated by foreigners who have their seats of authority in foreign lands, for example, French West Africa, French Equatorial Africa, Nigeria, Sierra Leone, Gambia, Belgian Congo, Portuguese Guinea, Basutoland, Swaziland and Bechuanaland.

(b) Those where indigenous Africans are dominated and oppressed by foreigners who have settled permanently in Africa and who regard the position of Africa under their sway as belonging more to them than to Africa, e.g. Kenya, Union of South Africa, Algeria, Rhodesia, Angola and Mozambique.

(3) Whereas world opinion unequivocally condemns oppression and subjugation of one race by another in whatever shape or form.

(4) Whereas all African peoples everywhere strongly deplore the economic exploitation of African peoples by imperialist countries thus reducing Africans to poverty in the midst of plenty.

(5) Whereas all African peoples vehemently resent the militarisation of Africans and the use of African soldiers in a nefarious global game against their brethren as in Algeria, Kenya, South Africa, Cameroons, Ivory Coast, Rhodesia and in the Suez Canal invasion.

(6) Whereas fundamental human rights, freedom of speech, freedom of association, freedom of movement, freedom of worship, freedom to live a full and abundant life, as approved by the All-African People's Conference on 13th December, 1958, are denied to Africans through the activities of imperialists.

(7) Whereas denial of the franchise to Africans on the basis of race or sex has been one of the principal instruments of colonial policy by imperialists and their agents, thus making it feasible for a few white settlers to lord it over millions of indigenous Africans as in the proposed Central African Federation, Kenya, Union of South Africa, Algeria, Angola, Mozambique and the Cameroons.

(8) Whereas imperialists are now coordinating their activities by forming military and economic pacts such as NATO, European Common Market, Free Trade Area, Organisation for European Economic Co-operation, Common Organisation in Sahara for the purpose of strengthening their imperialist activities in Africa and elsewhere,

Be it resolved and it is hereby resolved by; the All-African People's Conference meeting in Accra 5th to 13th December, 1958, and comprising over 300 delegates representing over 200 million Africans from all parts of Africa as follows:

1. That the All-African People's Conference vehemently condemns colonialism and imperialism in whatever shape or form these evils are perpetuated.

2. That the political and economic exploitation of Africans by imperialist Europeans should cease forthwith.

3. That the use of African manpower in the nefarious game of power politics by imperialists should be a thing of the past.

4. That independent African States should pursue in their international policy principles that will expedite and accelerate the independence and sovereignty of all dependent and colonial African territories.

5. That fundamental human rights be extended to all men and women in Africa and that the rights of indigenous Africans to the fullest use of their lands be respected and preserved.

6. That universal adult franchise be extended to all persons in Africa regardless of race or sex.

7. That independent African states ensure that fundamental human rights and universal adult franchise are fully extended to everyone within their states as an example to imperial nations who abuse and ignore the extension of those rights to Africans.

8. That a permanent secretariat of the All-African People's Conference be set up to organise the All-African Conference on a firm basis.

9. That a human rights committee of the Conference be formed to examine complaints of abuse of human rights in every part of Africa and to take appropriate steps to ensure the enjoyment of the rights by everyone.

10. That the All-African People's Conference in Accra declares its full support to all fighters for freedom in Africa, to all those who resort to peaceful means of non-violence and civil disobedience, as well as to all those who are compelled to retaliate against violence to attain national independence and freedom for the people. Where such retaliation becomes necessary, the Conference condemns all legislations which consider those who fight for their independence and freedom as ordinary criminals.

Questions

1. Why do the delegates object to imperialism and colonialism? Include four examples of things they oppose or condemn.

   a.

   b.

   c.

   d.

TRB 44 | Colonization and Independence in Africa
Day Five

Name:_____

2. a. How many delegates attended the conference?

   b. How many Africans did the delegates represent?

3. What do the delegates want for the future of Africa? Include four examples of the delegates' aspirations and demands.

   a.

   b.

   c.

   d.

4. According to section 10, what is the delegates' stance toward "fighters for freedom" in Africa? What does the resolution have to say about both nonviolent and violent efforts to achieve independence?

Name:_____

Colonization and Independence in Africa
Day Five
TRB 45

African Independence in the Twentieth Century

Instructions: Below is a chronology of African independence in the twentieth century. Using different colors, highlight the colonies according to their colonizing country (e.g. highlight all former British colonies yellow.) In cases where there is more than one colonizer, mark the most recent colonizing power. In the last column of the chart, fill in the number of countries that gained independence each year.

Year	Date	Colony	Colonizing Power	number/year
1922	February 28	Egypt	Britain	
1951	December 24	Libya	Italian colony until 1943, Britain/France '43-'51	
1952	September 11	Eritrea	Italian colony until 1941, Britain '41-'51	
1956	January 1	Sudan	Britain	
	March 2	Morocco	France	
	March 20	Tunisia	France	
	April 7	Northern Maurruecos	Spain	
	October 29	Tangier	Spain	
1957	March 6	Ghana	Britain	
1958	April 27	Southern Maurruecos	Spain	
	October 2	Guinea	France	
1960	January 1	Cameroon	France, Germany colony before WWI	
	April 27	Togo	France, Germany colony before WWI	
	June 20	Senegal	France	
		Mali	France	
	June 26	Madagascar	France	
		British Somaliland	Britain	
	June 30	Dem. Rep.of the Congo	Belgium	
	July 1	Somalia	Italy	
	August 1	Benin	France	
	August 3	Niger	France	
	August 5	Burkina Faso	France	
	August 7	Côte d'Ivoire	France	
	August 11	Chad	France	
	August 13	Central African Republic	France	
	August 15	Republic of the Congo	France	
	August 17	Gabon	France	
	October 1	Nigeria	Britain	
	November 28	Mauritania	France	

WWW.CHOICES.EDU ■ WATSON INSTITUTE FOR INTERNATIONAL STUDIES, BROWN UNIVERSITY ■ THE CHOICES PROGRAM

Year	Date	Country	Colonizer
1961	April 27	Sierra Leone	Britain
	June 1	British Cameroon North	Britain, German colony before WWI
	October 1	British Cameroon South	Britain, German colony before WWI
	December 9	Tanzania	Britain, German colony before WWI
1962	July 1	Burundi	Belgium, German colony before WWI
		Rwanda	Belgium, German colony before WWI
	July 3	Algeria	France
	October 9	Uganda	Britain
1963	December 10	Zanzibar	Britain
	December 12	Kenya	Britain
1964	July 6	Malawi	Britain
	October 24	Zambia	Britain
1965	February 18	Gambia	Britain
1966	September 30	Botswana	Britain
	October 4	Lesotho	Britain
1968	March 12	Mauritius	Britain
	September 6	Swaziland	Britain
	October 12	Equatorial Guinea	Spain
1969	June 30	Ifni	Spain
1974	September 10	Guinea Bissau	Portugal
1975	February 28	Western Sahara	Spain
	June 25	Mozambique	Portugal
	July 5	Cape Verde	Portugal
	July 6	Comoros	France
	July 12	São Tomé and Príncipe	Portugal
	November 11	Angola	Portugal
1976	June 26	Seychelles	Britain
1977	June 27	Djibouti	France
1980	April 18	Zimbabwe	Britain
1990	March 21	Namibia	South Africa, German colony before WWI
1994	April 27	South Africa	British until 1910, then white-majority rule until 1994

Name:_____

Colonization and
Independence in Africa
Day Five

TRB
47

Charting African Independence

Instructions: Use the information from the chronology to create a line graph representing the number of colonies that gained independence each year. Before adding the data points, be sure to label the x and y axes. Refer to the chronology and line graph to answer the questions below.

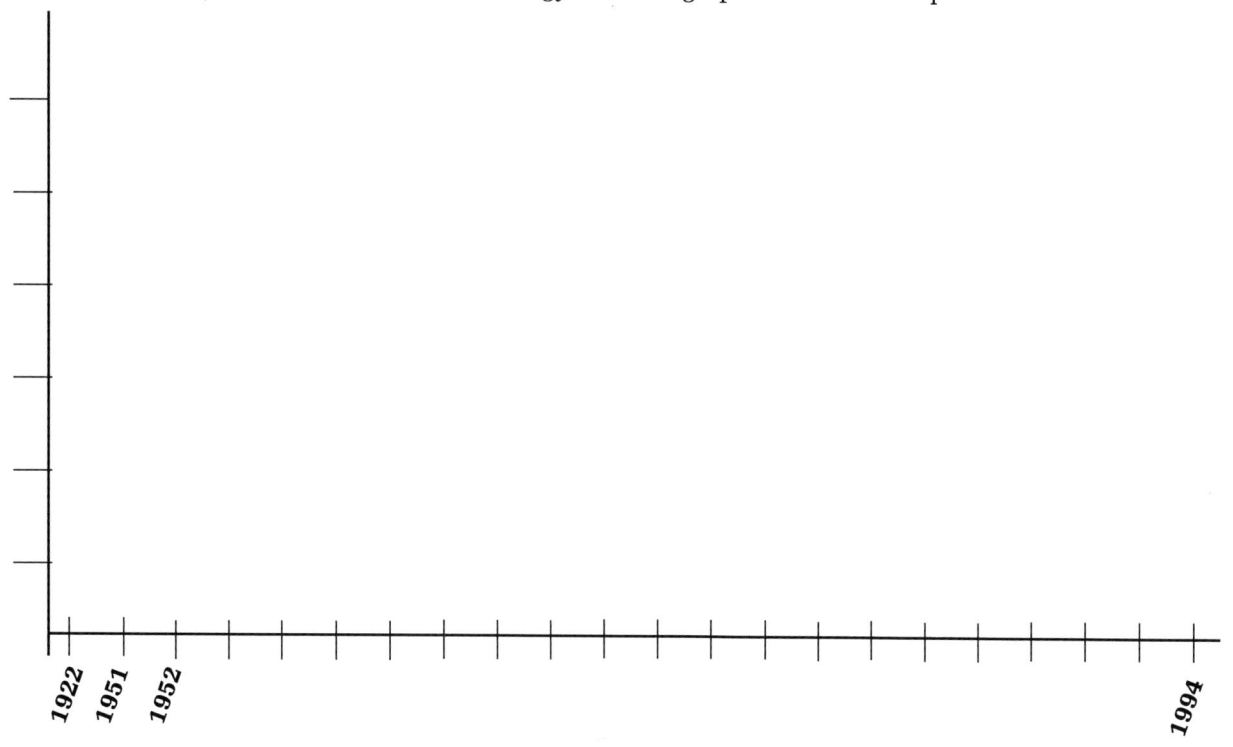

[Graph with x-axis labeled 1922, 1951, 1952, ... 1994]

Questions:
1. a. How many colonies became independent during the first half of the twentieth century?

   b. During the second half?

2. In what year did the majority of French colonies gain independence?

3. Circle the year of the All-African People's Conference on the line graph.
   a. What do you observe about the data for this year? What general observations can you make for the years before and after the conference?

   b. Write two questions you would want to research to better understand the data points for the years surrounding the conference.

WWW.CHOICES.EDU ■ WATSON INSTITUTE FOR INTERNATIONAL STUDIES, BROWN UNIVERSITY ■ THE CHOICES PROGRAM

Assessment Using Documents

Instructions: These questions relate to education policies during the colonial period in Africa.

1. a. In Document 1, what does Walter Rodney mean when he says that colonial education aimed to "instill a sense of deference towards all that was European and capitalist"?

   b. According to Rupert Emerson in Document 2, how did colonial education encourage African struggles for freedom?

2. How do Document 1 and Document 7 support the conclusions made in Document 4?

3. Assess the value and limitations of Document 6 and Document 8 for historians assessing the aims of colonial education policies. Be sure to refer to the origin and purpose of each document.

4. Using these sources and your knowledge, explain whether colonial education had a positive or negative effect on Africans.

Name:_____

Colonization and
Independence in Africa
Assessment

TRB
49

Documents

Document 1: Walter Rodney, *How Europe Underdeveloped Africa*, Howard University Press, 1982, pp. 240-241. Walter Rodney was a historian and political activist from Guyana.

> *"The colonizers did not introduce education into Africa: they introduced a new set of formal educational institutions which partly supplemented and partly replaced those which were there before.... The main purpose of the colonial school system was to train Africans to help man the local administration at the lowest ranks and to staff the private capitalist firms owned by Europeans.... It was not an educational system that grew out of the African environment or one that was designed to promote the most rational use of material and social resources. It was not an educational system designed to give young people confidence and pride as members of African societies, but one which sought to instill a sense of deference towards all that was European and capitalist."*

Document 2: Rupert Emerson, *From Empire to Nation: The Rise to Self-Assertion of Asian and African Peoples,* Harvard University Press, 1960, p. 53. Rupert Emerson was a professor of political science and international relations at Harvard University from 1927-1970.

> *"The few in the colonies with a Western type of education were well-prepared to receive Wilsonian doctrines of democracy and the right of people to govern themselves.... Colonial educational systems have frequently been attacked, with evident justice, for teaching the history of the metropolitan country or of Europe rather than local history—the stock image is that of children of French Africa or Madagascar reciting 'nos ancêstres les Gaulois' ('our ancestors the Gauls'*)—but it was from European history that the lessons of the struggle for freedom could on the whole be most effectively learned. The knowledge of Western languages opened up vast bodies of literature teeming with seditious thoughts which the young men who came upon them were not slow to apply to their own problems."*

* the Gauls are ancestors of the French

Document 3: Georges Nzongola-Ntalaja, *The Congo from Leopold to Kabila: A People's History*, Zed Books, 2002, pp. 78-79. Georges Nzongola-Ntalaja is a professor of African and Afro-American studies at the University of North Carolina at Chapel Hill.

> "In his otherwise excellent study of national independence movements in Asia and Africa, Rupert Emerson asserts that colonialism was a school for democracy—when in fact it was a school for tyranny—and that the largely illiterate masses had no clear understanding of the notion of people's sovereignty.... For him, only educated elites were in a position to understand such issues.... Anticolonial resistance in the Belgian Congo...was a resistance in which the masses, led by traditional rulers and organic intellectuals from their own ranks, took the initiative in fighting against the colonial system. And they did this without the benefit of knowledge derived from the Western classics, for the ideas of freedom and democracy are universal, and not an exclusive monopoly of the West.... No great intellectual exercise was required for ordinary people to reject colonialism and to yearn for a better political order."

Document 4: A. Adu Boahen, *African Perspectives on Colonialism*, The Johns Hopkins Press, 1987, p. 106. A. Adu Boahen was a Ghanaian historian and politician. He was an academic at the University of Ghana from 1959-1990, co-founder of the Movement for Freedom and Justice, and nominee of the New Patriotic Party in Ghana's 1992 presidential election.

> "The effects of colonial education were really unfortunate. First, because of its inadequacy, large numbers of Africans remained illiterate.... Secondly, the elite produced by these colonial educational institutions were with few exceptions people who were alienated from their own society in terms of their dress, outlook, and tastes in food, music, and even dance. They were people who worshipped European culture, equating it with civilization, and looked down upon their own culture. Radical African scholars are now talking of colonial miseducation rather than education. Unfortunately, it is this very alienated and badly oriented elite that have dominated both the political and the social scene in Africa since independence...."

Name:_____

Colonization and Independence in Africa
Assessment

TRB **51**

Document 5: From Donald Rothchild, *Racial Bargaining in Independent Kenya: A Study of Minorities and Decolonization*, Oxford University Press, 1973, p. 57.

Statistics: Kenya: Government Expenditure on Education, 1936

	European students	Asian students	African students
Government Expenditure	£49,814	£39,977	£80,721
Number of Pupils	1,889	7,996	100,720
Expenditure per Pupil	£26, 7 shillings, 5 pence	£5	16 shillings
Percent of Total Education Expenditure	29.2%	23.5%	47.3%

In this table, "Asian" is used to refer to people of Indian descent.

£ is the symbol for the British currency, the pound. There were 20 shillings in a pound, 12 pence in a shilling.

Document 6: Image from the French National Archives.

Caption: "A French school for girls in Algiers, the capital of Algeria."

The map in the photograph shows North Africa and the Mediterranean Sea. On the blackboard, a phrase in French states "The principle of wisdom is the fear of God."

Felix Jacques Antoine Moulin, Archives nationale d'outre-mer, 8Fi427/28.

Document 7: John D. Hargreaves, *Decolonization in Africa*, Addison Wesley Longman Limited, 1996, p. 68. John Hargreaves was a professor of history at the University of Aberdeen in Scotland from 1954-1985.

❝*By appointing two high-level Commissions in 1943 the (British) Colonial Office recognized that the foundation of African universities would form an essential part of their long-term preparations for gradual transfers of power. Besides acting as local centres of research and enquiry, their role would be to educate, not only cadres of administrators and professional specialists, but also political leaders.... [I]f the colonies were to evolve towards modern statehood the preparation of the inheritors would clearly be crucially important.... [T]he decisive test of this exercise in building African nation-states on European models would be the extent to which the values and interests of future rulers harmonized with those of their British peers.*❞

Document 8: Martin Schlunk, "The School System in the German Protectorates" (1914) in Bruce Fetter (ed.), *Colonial Rule in Africa: Readings from Primary Sources*, The University of Wisconsin Press, 1979, p. 126. Martin Schlunk was a leading German Protestant missionary in the early twentieth century. Schlunk based his article "The School System in the German Protectorates" on his analysis of a questionnaire sent to all German schools in Africa in 1911, at the request of the German Colonial Institute.

❝*[I]t is the duty of all the colonial schools to foster a feeling of loyalty on the part of the natives toward Germany and the German people.... [I]f Germany is to have colonies, and she must have them in order to live, every school must become an instrument of indoctrination of obedience for the German Reich and its rulers. But German language instruction is not absolutely essential here. It could help, but on the other hand, it could also have the opposite effect, since it would enable the natives to read all that undesirable literature which preaches internationalism instead of patriotism.... I am convinced that we shall have grave racial problems in our colonies in a few decades. It is absurd to think that even German-speaking natives will then be on our side. They will remain children of their culture whether they have learned to speak German or not. On the contrary, those natives who have received an education from us will then become leaders of their people in the struggle against us.*❞

Key Terms

Introduction and Part I
colonialism
colonial system
economic development
culture
agriculturalists
sovereignty
trade routes
exported
textiles
abolition
ideologies
ethnicities
treaties
missionary
guerilla warfare
cash crops
infrastructure
assimilation
indirect rule

Part II
anticolonial
nationalism
migrated
traditional leaders
blockade
conscripted
subsistence farming
fascism
self-determination
United Nations
the Cold War
authoritarian

Epilogue
legacies
elites
international relations
majority rule
apartheid
Non-Aligned Movement

Issues Toolbox

Sovereignty

Sovereignty is the absolute right of a state to govern itself. The United Nations (UN) Charter prohibits interference in the internal affairs of a sovereign state without the state's consent. Throughout human history, powerful states controlled the affairs of weaker states. Often accompanied by military conquest, this control was direct (for example, the colonization of large areas of Europe and Africa by the Roman Empire) or indirect (for example, the tributary states of the Aztec Empire). Even after the founding of the UN in 1945, powerful nations continued to use their international influence to define sovereignty to their advantage. In order to defend colonialism, they argued that sovereignty was something that colonial nations had to earn, rather than something that was their right. The successful lobbying of newly independent nations from places like Asia, Africa, and the Middle East in the mid-twentieth century shifted the balance of power in the international community, and gave rise to the more inclusive definition of sovereignty that we use today.

Nationalism

Nationalism is a strong devotion and loyalty to the interests of one's country and people. In the case of African anticolonial movements in the twentieth century, nationalism was a broad term used to describe the desire for African independence from European influence and control. After independence, new African leaders faced the significant task of fostering unity and loyalty among the diverse groups within their borders. The idea that someone was "Kenyan" or "Angolan"—what we consider nationalism today—was something that African leaders developed in the early years of independence.

Imperialism

Imperialism is the policy of extending the rule of a country over foreign countries. This can include acquiring colonies and dependencies. Imperialism has traditionally involved power and the use of coercion, whether military force or some other form. Colonialism is a form of imperialism, but imperialism is a broader concept that includes a wide array of policies that powerful states use to influence the affairs of weaker states. Like imperialism in other parts of the world, European imperialism in Africa was fueled by economics, racism, security, and religious or moral arguments. Many Europeans argued that they were spreading "civilization," in the form of European economic and political systems, religions, and culture. Imperialism in Africa did not end when African countries gained their independence. Through trade agreements, loans, military intervention, and diplomatic pressure, the colonial powers, along with the United States and the Soviet Union, continued to influence the affairs of African countries in the decades after independence.

Race

The idea that humans are divided into biologically distinct "races" that are identifiable by physical characteristics and innate behaviors has been proven false by historians, anthropologists, and biologists. But in the late nineteenth century, European leaders justified their colonization of the African continent by claiming that they belonged to a biologically and scientifically superior "race." They also used these ideas to justify their oppression of African people. For example, Europeans passed discriminatory legislation to limit the rights and privileges of Africans, and encouraged Africans to change their religion, language, and culture to be more European.

Making Choices Work in Your Classroom

This section of the Teacher Resource Book offers suggestions for teachers as they adapt Choices curricula on historical turning points to their classrooms. They are drawn from the experiences of teachers who have used Choices curricula successfully in their classrooms and from educational research on student-centered instruction.

Managing the Choices Simulation

A central activity of every Choices unit is the role-play simulation. Just as thoughtful preparation is necessary to set the stage for cooperative group learning, careful planning for the presentations can increase the effectiveness of the simulation. Time is the essential ingredient to keep in mind. A minimum of forty-five to fifty minutes is necessary for the presentations. Teachers who have been able to schedule a double period or extend the length of class to one hour report that the extra time is beneficial. When necessary, the role-play simulation can be run over two days, but this disrupts momentum. The best strategy for managing the role play is to establish and enforce strict time limits, such as five minutes for each presentation, ten minutes for questions and challenges, and the final five minutes of class for wrapping up. It is crucial to make students aware of strict time limits as they prepare their presentations. Our short video for teachers "Tips for a Successful Role Play" <www.choices.edu/pd/roleplay.php> also offers many helpful suggestions.

Adjusting for Students of Differing Abilities

Teachers of students at all levels—from middle school to AP—have used Choices materials successfully. Many teachers make adjustments to the materials for their students. Here are some suggestions:

- Go over vocabulary and concepts with visual tools such as concept maps and word pictures.
- Require students to answer guiding questions in the text as checks for understanding.
- Shorten reading assignments; cut and paste sections.
- Combine reading with political cartoon analysis, map analysis, or movie-watching.
- Read some sections of the readings out loud.
- Ask students to create graphic organizers for sections of the reading, or fill in ones you have partially completed.
- Supplement with different types of readings, such as short stories or news articles.
- Ask student groups to create a bumper sticker, PowerPoint presentation, or collage representing their case study.
- Do only some activities and readings from the unit rather than all of them.

Adjusting for Large and Small Classes

Choices units are designed for an average class of twenty-five students. In larger classes, additional roles, such as those of newspaper reporter or member of a special interest group, can be assigned to increase student participation in the simulation. With larger groups, additional tasks might be to create a poster, political cartoon, or public service announcement. In smaller classes, administrators, parents, or faculty can be invited to participate. Another option is to combine two small classes.

Assessing Student Achievement

Grading Group Assignments: Students and teachers both know that group grades can be motivating for students, while at the same time they can create controversy. Telling students in advance that the group will receive one grade often motivates group members to hold each other accountable. This can foster group cohesion and lead to better group results. It is also important to give individual grades for group work assignments in order to recognize an individual's contribution to the group. The "Assessment Guide for Oral Presentations" on the following page is designed to help teachers evaluate group presentations.

Requiring Self-Evaluation: Having students complete self-evaluations is an effective way to encourage them to think about their own learning. Self-evaluations can take many forms and are useful in a variety of circumstances. They are particularly helpful in getting students to think constructively about group collaboration. In developing a self-evaluation tool for students, teachers need to pose clear and direct questions to students. Two key benefits of student self-evaluation are that it involves students in the assessment process, and that it provides teachers with valuable insights into the contributions of individual students and the dynamics of different groups. These insights can help teachers to organize groups for future cooperative assignments.

Testing: Teachers say that students using the Choices approach learn the factual information presented as well as or better than from lecture-discussion format. Students using Choices curricula demonstrate a greater ability to think critically, analyze multiple perspectives, and articulate original viewpoints. Teachers should hold students accountable for learning historical information and concepts presented in Choices units. A variety of testing questions and assessment devices can be used to draw upon students' critical thinking and historical understanding.

For Further Reading

Daniels, Harvey, and Marilyn Bizar. *Teaching the Best Practice Way: Methods That Matter, K-12.* Portland, Maine: Stenhouse Publishers, 2005.

Assessment Guide for Oral Presentations

*Group assignment:*_____

*Group members:*_____
_____

Group Assessment	*Excellent*	*Good*	*Average*	*Needs Improvement*	*Unsatisfactory*
1. The group made good use of its preparation time	5	4	3	2	1
2. The presentation reflected analysis of the issues under consideration	5	4	3	2	1
3. The presentation was coherent and persuasive	5	4	3	2	1
4. The group incorporated relevant sections of the reading into its presentation	5	4	3	2	1
5. The group's presenters spoke clearly, maintained eye contact, and made an effort to hold the attention of their audience	5	4	3	2	1
6. The presentation incorporated contributions from all the members of the group	5	4	3	2	1

Individual Assessment					
1. The student cooperated with other group members	5	4	3	2	1
2. The student was well-prepared to meet their responsibilities	5	4	3	2	1
3. The student made a significant contribution to the group's presentation	5	4	3	2	1

Alternative Three-Day Lesson Plan

Day 1:
See Day Two of the Suggested Five-Day Lesson Plan. (Students should have read Part II of the reading and completed "Study Guide—Part II" or "Advanced Study Guide—Part II" before beginning the lesson. To gain an introduction to the topic, students should also read the Introduction.)

Homework: Students should read "Case Studies in Brief" and "Case Studies" in the student text.

Day 2:
Assign each student one of the four case studies, and allow students a few minutes to familiarize themselves with them. What is the central question of each assigned case? What were some European views on the central question? What were some African views?

Homework: Students should read "Epilogue: African Independence" and complete "Study Guide—Epilogue" or "Advanced Study Guide—Epilogue."

Day 3:
See Day Five of the Suggested Five-Day Lesson Plan.